Discovering EGYPTIANS

Richard Platt

Illustrations by L. R. Galante and Andrea Orani

ReD
KiTE

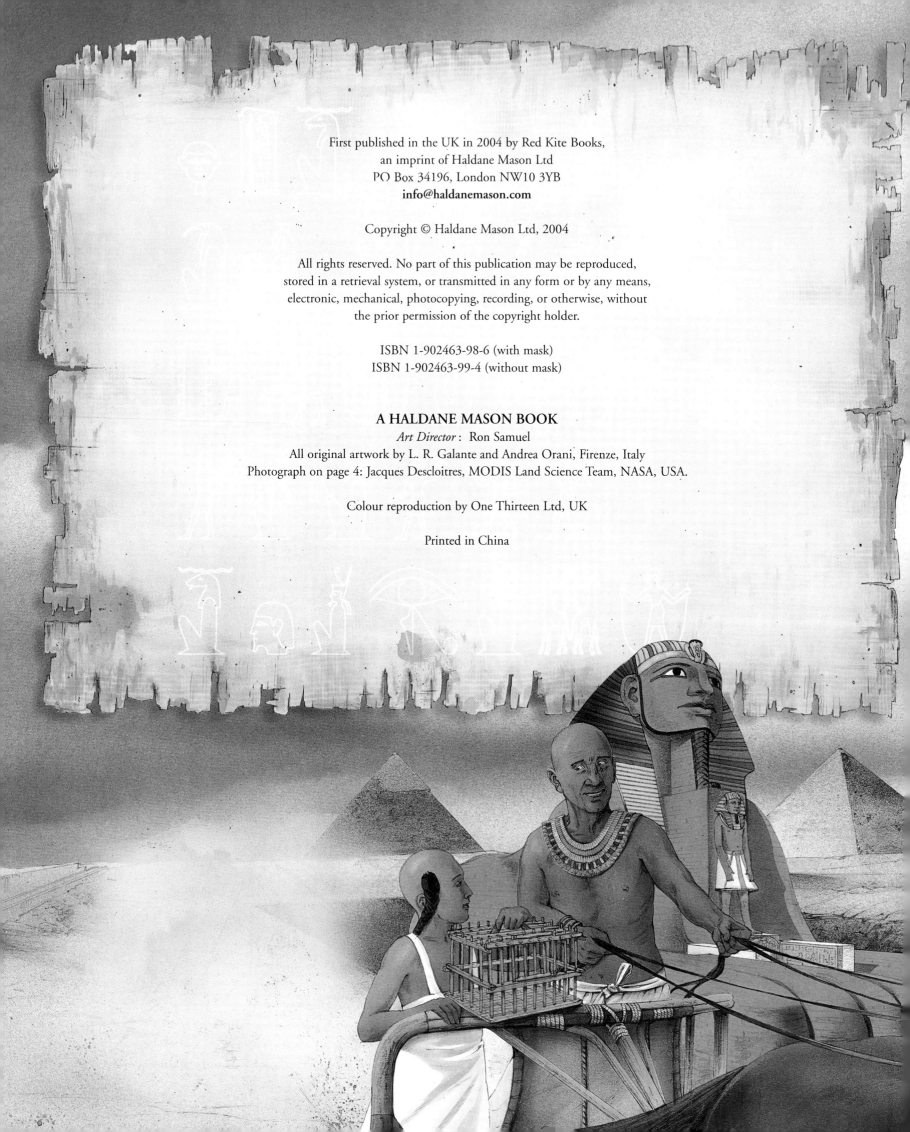

First published in the UK in 2004 by Red Kite Books,
an imprint of Haldane Mason Ltd
PO Box 34196, London NW10 3YB
info@haldanemason.com

ISBN 1-902463-98-6 (with mask)
ISBN 1-902463-99-4 (without mask)

A HALDANE MASON BOOK
Art Director : Ron Samuel
All original artwork by L. R. Galante and Andrea Orani, Firenze, Italy
Photograph on page 4: Jacques Descloitres, MODIS Land Science Team, NASA, USA.

Colour reproduction by One Thirteen Ltd, UK

Printed in China

Contents

The Black Land

An ancient kingdom that lasted for 3,000 years. A place of mystery, magic signs and golden treasures. A land of burning heat, choking sand – and lush green fields and cool waters. Ancient Egypt was all these things, and much more.

Seen from space, the Nile valley forms a ribbon of green in Africa's brown top-right corner. It wasn't always like this: 12,000 years ago the whole region was lush and green. However, the climate gradually became drier, and when people began to settle there 4,000 years later, the only land where plants would grow was the narrow strip flooded by the Nile each year.

On this strip, which its people called the 'black land', crops grew fast and fruitful. Thanks to abundant harvests, an advanced society grew up in Egypt. Working to plant and harvest crops and building ditches to water them drew the people of the valley together. By 3100 BC, the whole

▲ **The Nile valley:** seen from space, the green ribbon of the Nile snakes north across the sands of the Sahara Desert. The river flows out into the Mediterranean Sea through the green Nile delta. The stretch of water on the right is the Red Sea.

of Egypt was controlled by a single ruler, later called a pharaoh. Never before had a king or queen ruled over a whole land in this way.

Under the pharaoh's control, Egypt thrived. Officials organized farms, taking much of the farmers' grain harvest as tax. Some of the grain was carefully stored as a safeguard against famine. Some helped pay for building palaces and temples. In the temples, priests worshipped the pharaoh, and the many gods who they believed controlled the land of Egypt. The priests also devised a calendar to count the days and years. Scribes – professional writers – employed by the pharaoh kept government records in a language of pictures called hieroglyphs. Egyptian

craftsmen learned to make tools and weapons of metal. And, most of the time at least, the people of Egypt enjoyed peace and plenty.

Egyptians became so used to stability (freedom from chaos, and everything staying the same, year after year) that they had a special word for it: *maat*. One of the pharaoh's most important tasks was to make sure that *maat* did not end. Not all succeeded. There were some periods of chaos and war, no matter how hard the pharaohs tried to prevent them (see page 11). Eventually, Egypt was conquered and ruled by foreign peoples – first the Greeks, and then the Romans. But until these conquests brought Egyptian traditions to an end, life in the Nile valley continued with few major changes for nearly 3,000 years.

We know a lot about the Ancient Egyptians because

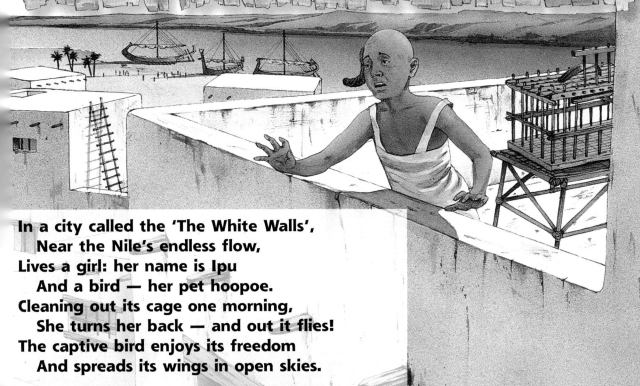

▾ **Egypt's towns:** the Nile Delta was called Lower Egypt, because it was lower on the river, and the country to the south, which was up-river, was called Upper Egypt. Once the country was united, pharaohs ruled from either Memphis or Thebes.

Mediterranean Sea
Rosetta
Nile Delta
Giza • Cairo
Saqqara
Memphis
Desert
Red Sea
Valley of the Kings • Karnak
Thebes
Edfu •
First Cataract •
River Nile
NUBIA Abu Simbel •

scarcely any rain falls on the country. Materials like cloth, paper and wood do not rot in the dry climate. Paintings on the walls of monuments and buildings look almost as fresh as the day they were completed.

In particular, tombs (burial places) are very well preserved. The ancient Egyptians liked to bury their dead in style, sending them off with all the comforts they had enjoyed in life. The tombs of pharaohs contained fantastic treasures, such as the golden coffin of Tutankhamun, which was discovered as recently as 1922. The outsides of some tombs were just as astonishing as the inside. One of them, the Great Pyramid, still stands just outside Egypt's modern capital, Cairo. It is so vast that – like the Nile valley itself – it can be seen from space with the naked eye.

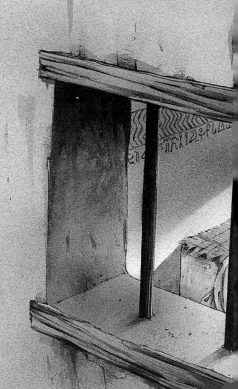

In a city called the 'The White Walls',
    Near the Nile's endless flow,
Lives a girl: her name is Ipu
    And a bird — her pet hoopoe.
Cleaning out its cage one morning,
    She turns her back — and out it flies!
The captive bird enjoys its freedom
    And spreads its wings in open skies.

The Nile

The river that watered and fertilized Egypt's fields also brought a regular rhythm to life. Each spring, the river rose, turning fields into lakes. The flood was so regular that the Egyptians based their calendar on its return.

To the Ancient Egyptians, the Nile was *iterw* – the river. Every April, regularly as clockwork, the river level began to rise. Within two months, much of the Nile valley was under water. The river water soaked the ground. It also covered it with rich, black mud, which worked like a natural fertilizer.

As the water level went down, the farmers planted seeds in the muddy fields. The heat in the months that followed made plants grow quickly, producing bumper crops.

The flood was so important that it gave its name to the season: the Egyptians called the months of April to July *Akhet*: inundation or flood. They also had a flood god, Hapy, to whom they prayed for high water. Hapy was a god of plenty, shown as a fat man with river weed for hair.

▲ **Shaduf:** the heavy weight on the end of the shaduf's swinging pole lifted the full bucket on the other end. This greatly reduced the work needed to water the fields.

In early Egyptian history, farmers cultivated only the areas of land that were naturally flooded by the river. But as time went on, they learned how to water fields farther from the banks, by raising dykes (earth walls) and digging canals (water channels). These had a gentle downward slope, so that water flowed along them. Later still they used the shaduf, a bucket hanging from a raised pole, to lift water from the river to higher fields. With the help of the shaduf, they could grow two crops a year.

The first of these crops was grain: the fields turned green and then golden yellow with wheat and barley. The grain was harvested with copper or flint-edged reaping hooks. Then the Egyptians

Dashing from the house she rushes
　　To the river at top speed.
Then running on the canal dykes
　　She sees the bird perched on a reed.
Lurking in the muddy water
　　A crocodile shows its shiny head.
His jaws snap shut, but Ipu's nimble
　　The croc bites on the wood instead.

threshed it (separated the edible grain from other parts of the plant) by walking their cattle on it. Farmers also grew the flax plant as a main crop, extracting linen fibre from its stems to weave into fabrics. The second crop was usually a vegetable: asparagus, beans, cabbage, cucumber, garlic, leek, lentils, lettuce, onions, peas, or radish.

The Nile's flood affected every part of life in the valley. The mud hid field

▸ **Nilometer:** to measure the height of the Nile's floods, Egyptian priests used a device that looked very like a staircase. Counting the submerged steps showed roughly how deep the water was; grooves carved on the wall made the measurement exact.

Astronomy

Egyptian priests used astronomy (the study of the stars' movement) to help predict the Nile's flood. The flood was deepest when the brightest star, Sirius, first appeared on the horizon after months out of sight. By watching Sirius and timing its rising, the priests learned that the year was not exactly 365 days, but a quarter day longer. They also used astronomy to choose the exact position of sacred buildings.

▸ **Egyptian astronomers:** watching stars needed only simple instruments.

boundaries, so Egyptians became clever surveyors: field scribes (officials) had to measure and map the fields, then mark them out when the flood fell. Taxes were based on the Nile's level, for higher floods meant better harvests – and higher taxes. Tax scribes measured the flood with a staircase-like meter called a nilometer. The Nile's regular flood was also the origin of the world's first accurate calendar. Priests worked out the dates so that they could accurately predict when the river would rise again, years in advance.

Getting Around

Egypt's river was the main transport highway. Reed boats provided a quick, cheap way of making short journeys. Heavy loads travelled on huge barges – the equivalent of today's monster trucks.

Winding from the Mediterranean Sea in the north to the Nile's First Cataract (waterfall) in the south, Egypt was a long, snake-shaped country. Though narrow enough to walk across in an hour in some places, the black land was 1,200 km (750 miles) long, so transport was vitally important to its people.

Fortunately, the river provided a convenient (though not always quick) way to move around. Travelling north was easy: the river's current swept boats and ships downstream towards the Mediterranean Sea. All the boatmen had to do was steer. Drifting the 725 km (450 miles) between the country's two major cities, Thebes and Memphis, took about two weeks – less during flood season.

Going the other way was only a little more difficult. There was usually a wind from the north, so by hoisting a sail, mariners could use the wind to blow their ships back up the river. Ships used oars only when the wind dropped or when they had very urgent business.

The Nile bustled with vessels of all sizes. The biggest ships carried stone for building, and finished obelisks (stone columns). A few of these ships were as long as a soccer pitch, and weighed 7,300 tonnes. They were the biggest ships in the world at the time, and none was built bigger for another 3,300 years, until the big sailing ships of the eighteenth century.

▼ **Sedan chair:** pharaohs used sedan chairs on ceremonial occasions long after chariots replaced them for daily transport.

The hoopoe flies across the river
     To a tree the other side.
Ipu begs a gentle ferryman
     'Can't I have just one free ride?'
As soon as they have crossed the river
     Her feathered pet turns right around;
And rowing back across the water
     The ferryman almost runs aground.

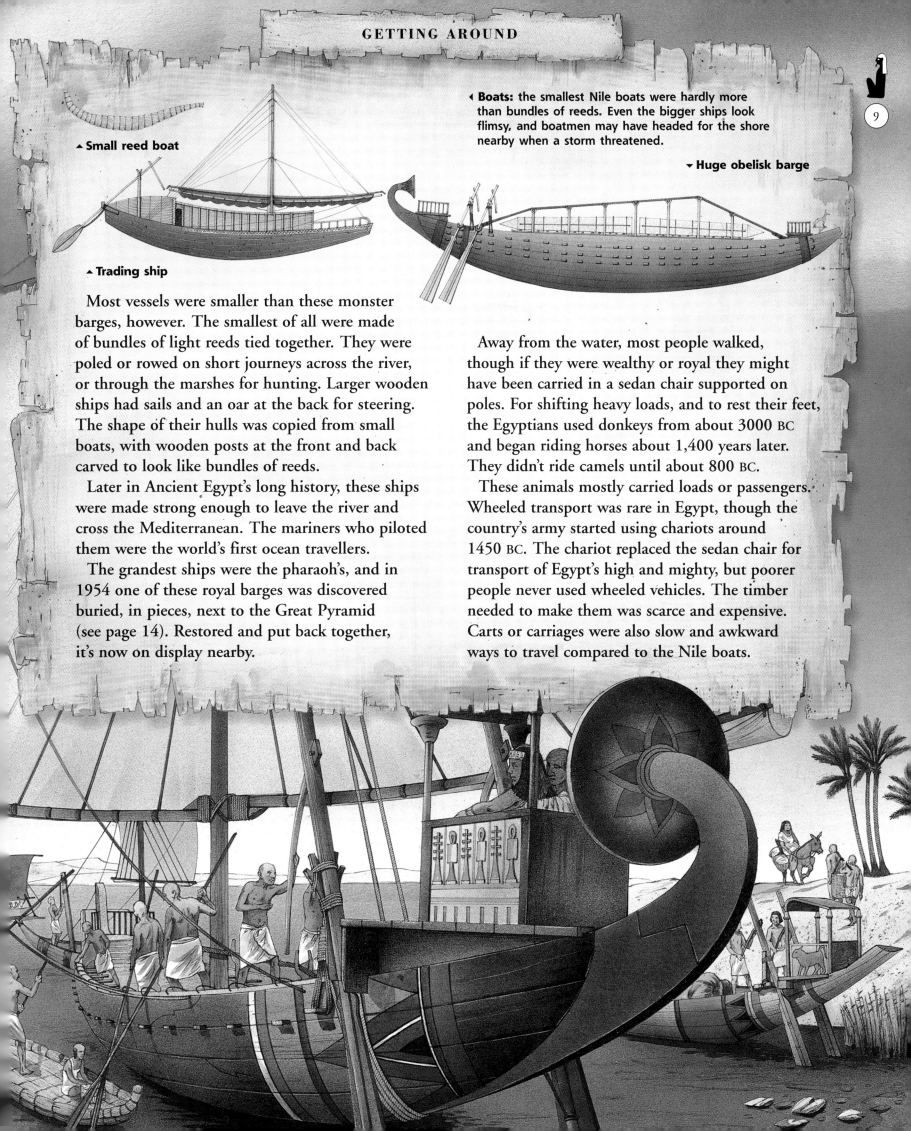

▲ Small reed boat

◀ **Boats:** the smallest Nile boats were hardly more than bundles of reeds. Even the bigger ships look flimsy, and boatmen may have headed for the shore nearby when a storm threatened.

▼ **Huge obelisk barge**

▲ **Trading ship**

Most vessels were smaller than these monster barges, however. The smallest of all were made of bundles of light reeds tied together. They were poled or rowed on short journeys across the river, or through the marshes for hunting. Larger wooden ships had sails and an oar at the back for steering. The shape of their hulls was copied from small boats, with wooden posts at the front and back carved to look like bundles of reeds.

Later in Ancient Egypt's long history, these ships were made strong enough to leave the river and cross the Mediterranean. The mariners who piloted them were the world's first ocean travellers.

The grandest ships were the pharaoh's, and in 1954 one of these royal barges was discovered buried, in pieces, next to the Great Pyramid (see page 14). Restored and put back together, it's now on display nearby.

Away from the water, most people walked, though if they were wealthy or royal they might have been carried in a sedan chair supported on poles. For shifting heavy loads, and to rest their feet, the Egyptians used donkeys from about 3000 BC and began riding horses about 1,400 years later. They didn't ride camels until about 800 BC.

These animals mostly carried loads or passengers. Wheeled transport was rare in Egypt, though the country's army started using chariots around 1450 BC. The chariot replaced the sedan chair for transport of Egypt's high and mighty, but poorer people never used wheeled vehicles. The timber needed to make them was scarce and expensive. Carts or carriages were also slow and awkward ways to travel compared to the Nile boats.

Pharaohs

Obeyed as a king and worshipped as a god, Egypt's pharaoh had absolute power over his people. The country was his, and he controlled everyone and everything in it. His people even believed that he had power over the natural world, ordering the Nile's flood and commanding crops to grow.

Pharaohs had quite a job to do: besides governing the country, they were also in charge of religion and the temples, of the army, and of law and order. But their most important job was to preserve *maat*. Though impossible to translate exactly, this word meant calmness and stability, or the unchanging, continuous nature of Egypt.

Most pharaohs were men, but not all of them. In the 18th dynasty, Queen Hatshepsut ruled the country. However, in keeping with tradition, she dressed as a man – right down to the false beard that pharaohs wore for state ceremonies!

◀ **Chariot:** skilfully used, and with an expert driver, the chariot was a terror weapon. It was as frightening in its day as tanks are now.

Ruling the country was a family business. When a pharaoh died, his son took over the throne, and with it, the pharaoh's magical abilities. The serpent on his crown was a sign of these powers. Called the *uraeus*, it was believed to spit fire at his foes.

When neighbouring nations threatened Egypt, the pharaoh – with the *uraeus* on his crown – led his troops into battle. His soldiers fought with simple axes, clubs, daggers, bows and spears. They wore no armour, fighting almost naked, and protecting themselves only with shields and helmets. Battle was a grisly business: when they

The bird flies low above the city
  Calling out its hooting song.
But there's a louder, prouder sound
  As squads of soldiers march along.
The Pharaoh leads a thousand warriors
  Returning from a bloody war.
Cheering crowds block off the street —
  And Ipu's bird escapes once more.

Dynasties and Kingdoms

Ancient Egyptian history spans some 3,000 years, from when the whole country was first ruled by a single king to roughly the time our own calendar began 2,000 years ago. Historians divide this time into some 30 dynasties. The rulers in each dynasty came from the same family. Dynasties are grouped into kingdoms. Most of the pyramids were built during the Old Kingdom (2686–2181 BC). The Middle Kingdom (2134–1784 BC) strengthened the power of the pharaoh after a short period of chaos called the First Intermediate Period. More confusion followed, but in the New Kingdom (1570–1069 BC) Egypt was again united, and conquered neighbouring countries.

3100 BC	2686 BC	2181 BC 2134 BC	1784 BC	1570 BC	1069 BC	664 BC	332–30 BC
Early Dynastic Period	OLD KINGDOM	MIDDLE KINGDOM First Intermediate Period	Second Intermediate Period	NEW KINGDOM	Third Intermediate Period	Late Period	Ptolemaic Period

◀ **Structure of society:** The pharaoh's wealthy relations helped the viziers rule the country. Scribes organized everything, like today's government officials. Huge numbers of peasant farmers grew the corn that fed the wealthy few who ruled them.

Pharaoh

**2 Viziers,
for Upper and
Lower Egypt**

Noble families

Scribes **Priests**

Craft workers

Ordinary people: farmers,
soldiers, labourers and servants

Slaves

killed an enemy warrior, Egyptian soldiers hacked off the right hand as a grim trophy – and to help count up the enemy dead. Killing wasn't the only aim, though. Captured foes became valuable slaves, and were shared out among the troops as a welcome bonus.

Egypt's soldiers had their share of victories and defeats, but from about 1450 BC a new invention made them much harder to beat. Around this time, craftsmen began making lightweight two-wheeled chariots. Pulled by a pair of horses, chariots carried a driver and an archer. These teams drove their chariots quickly towards the enemy army, showered them with arrows, and escaped just as quickly.

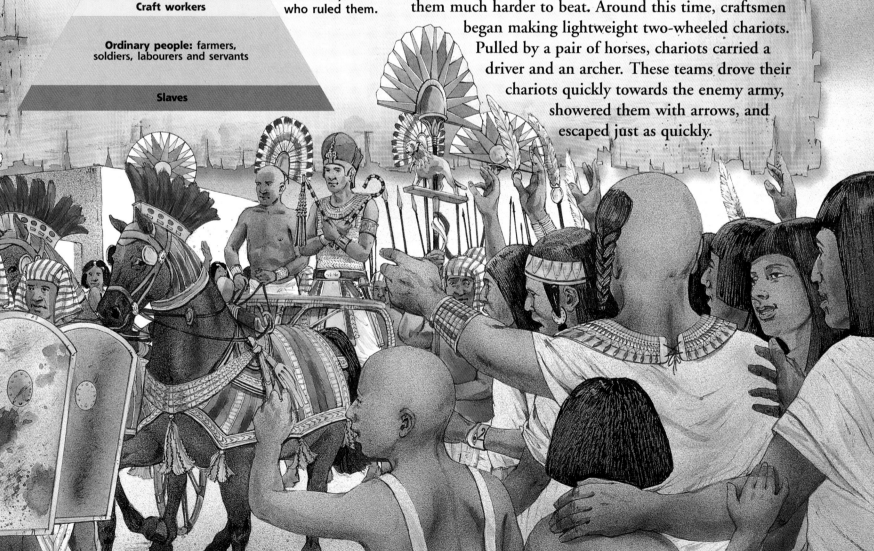

Everyday Life

*Wealthy Egyptians could afford beautiful jewellery and fashionable, clean clothes.
Peasant farmers weren't so lucky. They lived and worked half-naked. But whether
rich or poor, most people lived in simple rooms, for furniture was scarce.*

In Egypt's hot desert climate, people rarely needed clothes to protect themselves against the weather. Children went naked until they reached their teens, and river workers such as fishermen, boatmen and reed-gatherers also wore no clothes. Most other peasant workers wore a loin cloth. 'Dressing up' meant putting on a simple white linen kilt, and perhaps a loose-fitting shirt. Peasant women usually wore ankle-length white sleeveless dresses, though servants and dancers often went topless.

Wealthier Egyptians wore smarter clothes: men's kilts, for example, were pleated and crisply starched, and women wore long-sleeved gowns in the evenings. The rich could afford to change their clothes several times each day. They followed fashion, too, just as people do now. For example, at the time when

▲ **Dressing up:** gold was 'the flesh of the sun' and only noble families were allowed gold jewellery.

Rome ruled Egypt, smart women wore very fine, see-through fabrics.

Jewellery, wigs and make-up completed their outfits. Though styles changed constantly, wealthy people of both sexes wore elaborate jewellery round their necks, waists, arms and ankles (though not usually all at once). Jewellers fixed gems such as lapis lazuli, turquoise and amethyst into gold and silver settings. For cheaper pieces, they used faience, a kind of pottery with a brilliant blue glaze. Poorer women made do with a string of beads or even coloured ribbons.

Wigs, worn by both men and women, were signs of wealth. Cosmetics, on the other hand, weren't reserved for rich women – everyone wore eye make-up, even men. This wasn't just for vanity. The ground stone used in green make-up may have helped protect against eye

infections, and black helped block the sun's glare. Workers building the tomb of Pharaoh Rameses III even went on strike in 1158 BC because – besides being hungry – they had not received their rations of eye shadow!

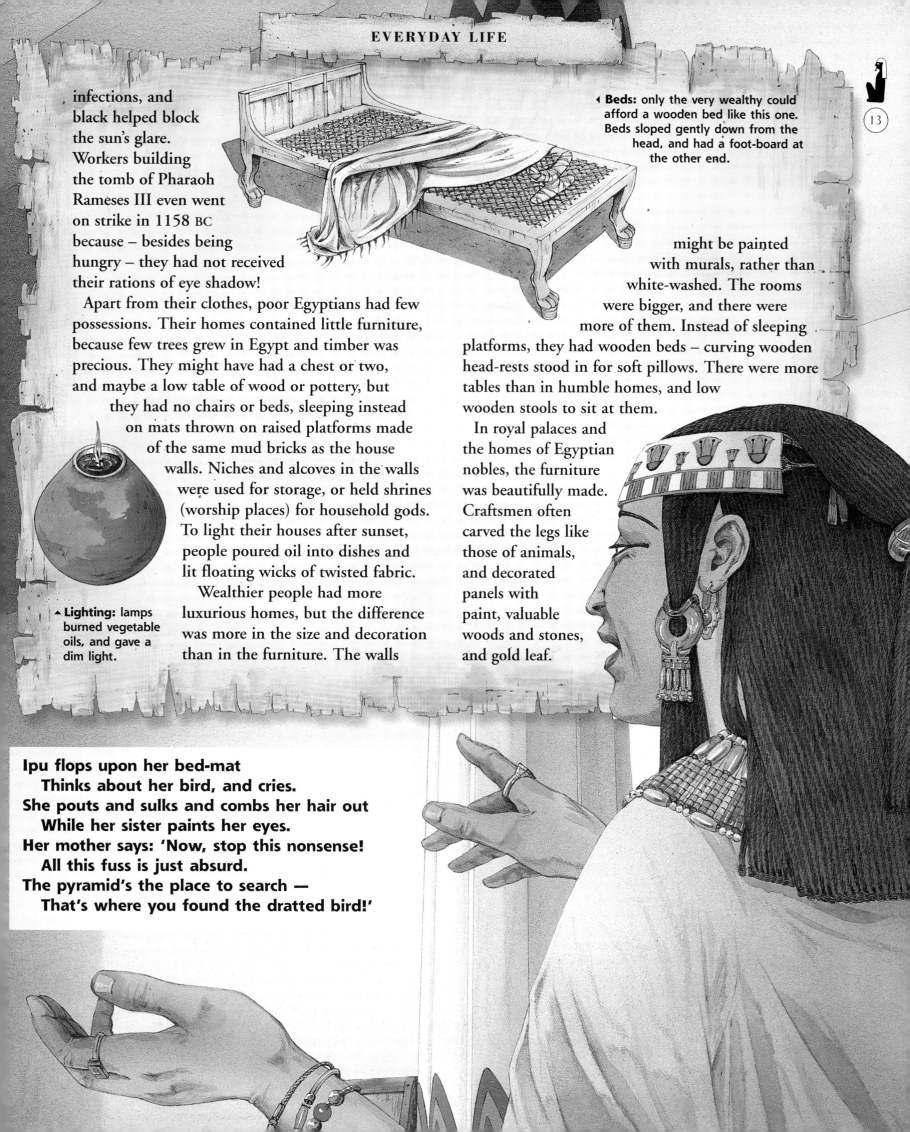

Beds: only the very wealthy could afford a wooden bed like this one. Beds sloped gently down from the head, and had a foot-board at the other end.

Apart from their clothes, poor Egyptians had few possessions. Their homes contained little furniture, because few trees grew in Egypt and timber was precious. They might have had a chest or two, and maybe a low table of wood or pottery, but they had no chairs or beds, sleeping instead on mats thrown on raised platforms made of the same mud bricks as the house walls. Niches and alcoves in the walls were used for storage, or held shrines (worship places) for household gods. To light their houses after sunset, people poured oil into dishes and lit floating wicks of twisted fabric.

Wealthier people had more luxurious homes, but the difference was more in the size and decoration than in the furniture. The walls

▲ **Lighting:** lamps burned vegetable oils, and gave a dim light.

might be painted with murals, rather than white-washed. The rooms were bigger, and there were more of them. Instead of sleeping platforms, they had wooden beds – curving wooden head-rests stood in for soft pillows. There were more tables than in humble homes, and low wooden stools to sit at them.

In royal palaces and the homes of Egyptian nobles, the furniture was beautifully made. Craftsmen often carved the legs like those of animals, and decorated panels with paint, valuable woods and stones, and gold leaf.

Ipu flops upon her bed-mat
  Thinks about her bird, and cries.
She pouts and sulks and combs her hair out
  While her sister paints her eyes.
Her mother says: 'Now, stop this nonsense!
  All this fuss is just absurd.
The pyramid's the place to search —
  That's where you found the dratted bird!'

Pyramids and Tombs

A gigantic triangle soaring high above Egypt's modern capital of Cairo, the Great Pyramid was built 4,570 years ago as a tomb for Pharaoh Khufu. Though it has been studied for centuries, it's still a mysterious structure with a power to astonish visitors.

Khufu's vast tomb is not the only pyramid in Egypt – nor was it the first. Egyptians began making these triangular graves around 2650 BC. At first, their sides were not plain triangles, but huge steps. In the vast necropolis (city of the dead) at Saqqara, you can still see the step pyramid of Djoser, who started the stone pyramid fashion. It continued for about ten centuries, and by its end, there were some 80 or so pyramids scattered along Egypt's desert edge.

Khufu's Great Pyramid stands at Giza, on the outskirts of modern-day Cairo. Alongside it are two smaller pyramids built for pharaohs who followed him, and miniature pyramids for their queens. Near by, gazing out across the Nile valley, crouches the Sphinx, a vast stone cat with the face of Pharaoh Khafre, who ruled Egypt some 30 years after Khufu.

▲ **Djoser's tomb:** as high as a 15-storey building, Djoser's stepped pyramid was Egypt's first. The pharaoh's tomb lay under it, at the bottom of a deep shaft.

Of all these buildings, Khufu's pyramid is by far the most famous, though it is only a camel's height taller than that of Khafre next door. Built from 2,300,000 limestone blocks, the Great Pyramid contains more stone than all the ancient cathedrals in Europe. Its sides, now jumbled staircases of blocks, once had a smooth cover of brilliant white sloping slabs. Builders took these long ago to construct walls in Cairo.

Inside, the pyramid contains not one but three burial chambers, constructed one after the other as plans changed. Narrow passages join them, and link them to the entrance. Two of these corridors are exactly aligned with stars that the Egyptians thought very important. This has led some experts to suggest that the pyramid was once used to watch the stars and time their movement. It's impossible

to prove this – or many of the other theories about why the pyramid was built.

The pyramid contains many other baffling riddles, and archaeologists are still discovering more. As recently as 2003, scientists sent a robot camera up an air-shaft in the pyramid. It revealed a mysterious new chamber, guarded by a door with twin copper handles.

Equally puzzling is the question of how the Great Pyramid was built. Archaeologists believe that the men of Egypt may have been forced to work on the pyramid while the Nile's annual flood stopped them farming. They guess that work-squads built ramps around the pyramid so that they could raise the 6,500,000 tonnes of stone needed to complete it.

This vast mass of stone was supposed to protect Khufu's burial, but it did not. Tomb robbers broke in, seeking the gold and precious objects surrounding the pharaoh. The pyramid has been empty for as long as people have been studying it.

Robbers broke into all the pyramids, and by the New Kingdom, Egypt's pharaohs were looking for a better way to protect their graves. They hit on the idea of hiding the tombs in lonely valleys. In the Valley of the Kings near Thebes, workers tunnelled 60 tombs into the solid rock. Even this did not keep the robbers out, and most were emptied of valuables. The only one that escaped destruction was that of Tutankhamun. When it was uncovered by English archaeologist Howard Carter in 1922, it contained astonishing, almost unspoiled treasures. This golden tomb gave the world a fascinating glimpse of the luxurious lives of the pharaohs and the richness of their deaths.

Entrance in the Valley of the Kings

Sloping corridors

Well chamber

Pillared chamber

Side chambers

Burial chamber

◄ **Tunnel tombs:** from about 1500 BC, the Egyptians began burying their pharaohs in tombs tunnelled into the solid rock of the Valley of the Kings. The small entrance in the valley wall led down steps to the burial room. This is the tomb of the great New Kingdom Pharaoh Rameses II.

Next day Ipu starts her search again
  She travels in her uncle's chariot.
She hands him up her hoopoe's cage.
  He says: 'I'm driving — you can carry it!'
The hoopoe's nowhere to be seen;
  They drive back past the old necropolis.
Among the graves a tomb stands high —
  The bird's perched out of reach on top of this.

Mummies

For the Ancient Egyptians, death was nothing to be feared: it was simply a short break in their lives. If they prepared carefully enough, and their families could afford to preserve their bodies, they were sure they could live again – forever.

Like many religious people today, Egyptians believed in the after-life, a place to which the dead travelled and enjoyed an everlasting new life of rest and pleasure. Reaching the afterlife was not easy, however. It required prayer, rituals (holy ceremonies), offerings to the gods and, most important of all, mummification. This was an embalming process that aimed to preserve the body – a difficult task in a hot climate, where meat quickly rots.

Embalmers offered their customers three different levels of service. Their cheapest method was simply to empty the gut, then cover the body in natron. This natural salt was dug from the desert. It was a mixture of the chemicals we now use as baking powder and washing soda.

▲ **Tutankhamun:** the tomb of this New Kingdom pharaoh contained many gold decorations of breathtaking beauty, including a life-size golden mask.

Over 40 days, it dried out the corpse – but left it black and twisted.

More costly methods aimed for better preservation: the embalmers could inject a chemical through the anus (bottom) which dissolved the guts. However, the very wealthy opted for a much more expensive solution. The embalmers started by scraping out the brains with a metal hook (they pushed this up the nose to avoid breaking the skin). Next, they neatly cut open the body with a special flint knife. They removed all the organs except the heart, washed the cavity and perfumed it with spices. This helped to slow the body's decay. The natron bath followed. Removed organs were preserved separately in special containers called canopic jars.

As the bird flies on, she follows
    Down dark lanes and through a gate.
When it darts into a courtyard,
    Ipu does not hesitate.
She pushes on an unlocked door —
    The room inside is black as night.
And blinking in the gloom she sees
    A human corpse, all wrapped up tight!

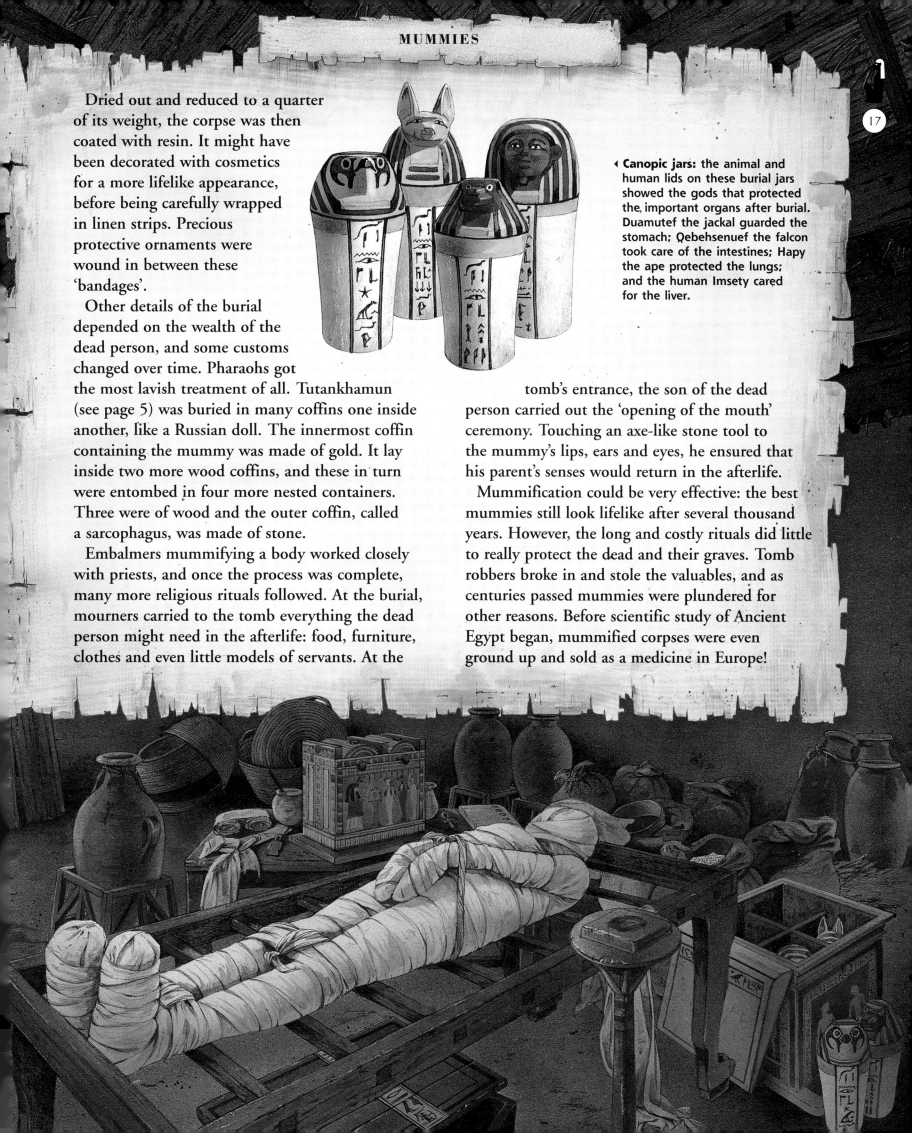

Dried out and reduced to a quarter of its weight, the corpse was then coated with resin. It might have been decorated with cosmetics for a more lifelike appearance, before being carefully wrapped in linen strips. Precious protective ornaments were wound in between these 'bandages'.

Other details of the burial depended on the wealth of the dead person, and some customs changed over time. Pharaohs got the most lavish treatment of all. Tutankhamun (see page 5) was buried in many coffins one inside another, like a Russian doll. The innermost coffin containing the mummy was made of gold. It lay inside two more wood coffins, and these in turn were entombed in four more nested containers. Three were of wood and the outer coffin, called a sarcophagus, was made of stone.

Embalmers mummifying a body worked closely with priests, and once the process was complete, many more religious rituals followed. At the burial, mourners carried to the tomb everything the dead person might need in the afterlife: food, furniture, clothes and even little models of servants. At the

◄ **Canopic jars:** the animal and human lids on these burial jars showed the gods that protected the important organs after burial. Duamutef the jackal guarded the stomach; Qebehsenuef the falcon took care of the intestines; Hapy the ape protected the lungs; and the human Imsety cared for the liver.

tomb's entrance, the son of the dead person carried out the 'opening of the mouth' ceremony. Touching an axe-like stone tool to the mummy's lips, ears and eyes, he ensured that his parent's senses would return in the afterlife.

Mummification could be very effective: the best mummies still look lifelike after several thousand years. However, the long and costly rituals did little to really protect the dead and their graves. Tomb robbers broke in and stole the valuables, and as centuries passed mummies were plundered for other reasons. Before scientific study of Ancient Egypt began, mummified corpses were even ground up and sold as a medicine in Europe!

Food and Drink

Delicacies such as braised ostrich, blood pudding and pigs' snouts added welcome variety to the diets of wealthy Egyptians, but peasant families had to make do with bread, beer and onions.

In normal years, the reliable Nile made sure that few people living on its banks went hungry. When low floods meant crops did not grow, government officials gave out food saved from better years. The reserve supplies were wheat or barley, for these were the main crops of the fertile Egyptian fields.

Turning these grains into a meal was a long, laborious task. To mill the grain into flour, women crushed it using a saddle quern (a low sloping stone slab) and a stone roller. Kneeling at one end, women used the roller much like a rolling pin to crush the grain until it was fine enough for baking. Making enough flour to feed a family for a day took one woman most of the day.

Mixing with water and adding yeast from beer-froth made a soft dough. Baked in a mould, or flat

◄ **Pressing grapes:** sweet grapes ripened fast in Egypt's hot climate. To make wine, workers crushed the grapes underfoot.

like pitta, the dough became a bread. Compared with our bread, Egyptian bread was coarse and heavy. It was gritty, too, as grains of sand crept in during harvesting, milling and baking. A lifetime of eating gritty bread ground down Egyptians' teeth to stumps.

Barley bread was turned into beer. Lightly-baked loaves were broken up and left to soak in water. Yeast in the bread turned some of the water to alcohol, producing a soupy, thick beer. It was often not very alcoholic, but getting drunk was not the main reason for drinking it: the beer was a high-energy food, and the brewing process helped purify the water used, so that beer was safer to

drink than water. Children drank it as well as adults: a scene painted on a New Kingdom tomb shows a child holding out a bowl, with the words 'give me some beer, for I am hungry'.

These two foods together made up the main diet of poor Egyptians, but were not the only foods the poor ate. They varied their diet with onions and other vegetables – especially beans, garlic, lettuce and cucumbers. They ate fruit such as dates, figs and grapes. They also caught fish from the Nile and trapped birds along its marshy banks. Few ate other meats except at festivals or celebrations.

Better-off Egyptians also ate pork, beef and game (hunted wild birds and beasts) such as gazelle and ostrich. In general, they had a richer and more interesting diet, though, like the poor, they ate a lot of bread, and their teeth suffered as a result, too.

The addition of honey, spices and fruit made the bread of the rich more tasty, and their brewers also used honey to sweeten their beer. When they tired of beer, they could drink wine. Too costly for the poor, it was stored in jars marked – like today's bottles – with the vineyard name and the year it was made.

Banquets

Though we know a lot about what people ate, it's more difficult to say how they cooked it, for no recipes have survived. Tomb paintings show cooks boiling, roasting and frying meat, but we can only guess at the flavour of the finished dishes. Tombs also record banquet scenes: the well-off guests sit at individual tables on mats or stools. There are flowers and crockery on the table, but no cutlery: diners eat with their fingers and servants wash them afterwards. Other servants bring food and pour wine, spray perfume, or entertain with music and dancing. Some guests didn't know when to stop: the tomb of Khety, a governor who lived some 4,000 years ago, shows enthusiastic party-goers carrying home their drunken friends.

▶ **Party animals:** just like today's parties, Egyptian banquets were a chance to swap gossip, meet friends, and compare the latest fashions.

Back at home she tells the slave girl
   Of the sight she saw — so shocking!
Then takes a turn at grinding corn,
   Making flour by gently rocking.
As they cook a meal together
   Her friend gives Ipu some advice:
'Why don't you try down at the temple;
   The priests and gods have helped me twice.'

Magic and Religion

From the pharaoh to the humblest slave, Egyptians believed that their world was under the control of the gods. Priests worshipped them in towering temples, and every mud-brick house had a shrine where the family prayed.

In a field of waving golden wheat, the pharaoh prays to Min, the god of fertility, and starts the harvest by cutting the first stalks. Then through the whole Nile valley farmers and slaves bringing in the crop beat their chests with their fists, in honour of Isis. This goddess, they believe, brings the seed grain to life and makes it grow.

Min and Isis were just two of the most important Egyptian gods, but there were dozens of others, and even more of the lesser gods. For religion, like the Nile, ran through everything in Egypt. Egyptians believed that the pharaoh himself was a god. As the head of the country's religion, it was his job to please all the other gods. Only by doing so could he preserve *maat* (see page 10) and stop chaos and disorder from destroying the country.

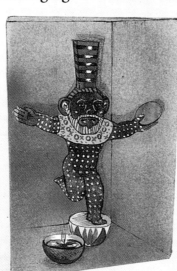

▲ **Household shrine:** in every home a small statue of a god stood in a red-painted hollow in the mud wall.

The pharaoh could not do this on his own. He was helped by many thousands of priests all around the country. The priests worked in grand temples. The size and stone walls of the temples made clear their importance (most other buildings apart from palaces were made from mud bricks). Their strong walls have ensured that, several thousands of years after they were built, some temples are still standing. The temple of Edfu, for example, is nearly complete.

Within each temple, priests worshipped a statue of their particular god. Some took human form: for example, Horus, guardian god of the pharaoh, was shown as a hawk, or a man with a hawk's head. Not all the gods had animal shapes. Hathor, the sky god shown in the temple below, was a woman – though she was often shown with cow's ears.

The priests are kind and listen well
   As Ipu tells them what she wants.
They pass her wish on to the idol;
   She waits in fear for the response.
The priest assures her Hathor's helpful
   And the truth she'll always tell.
The god's reply booms from the statue:
   'Seek in the place where workers dwell.'

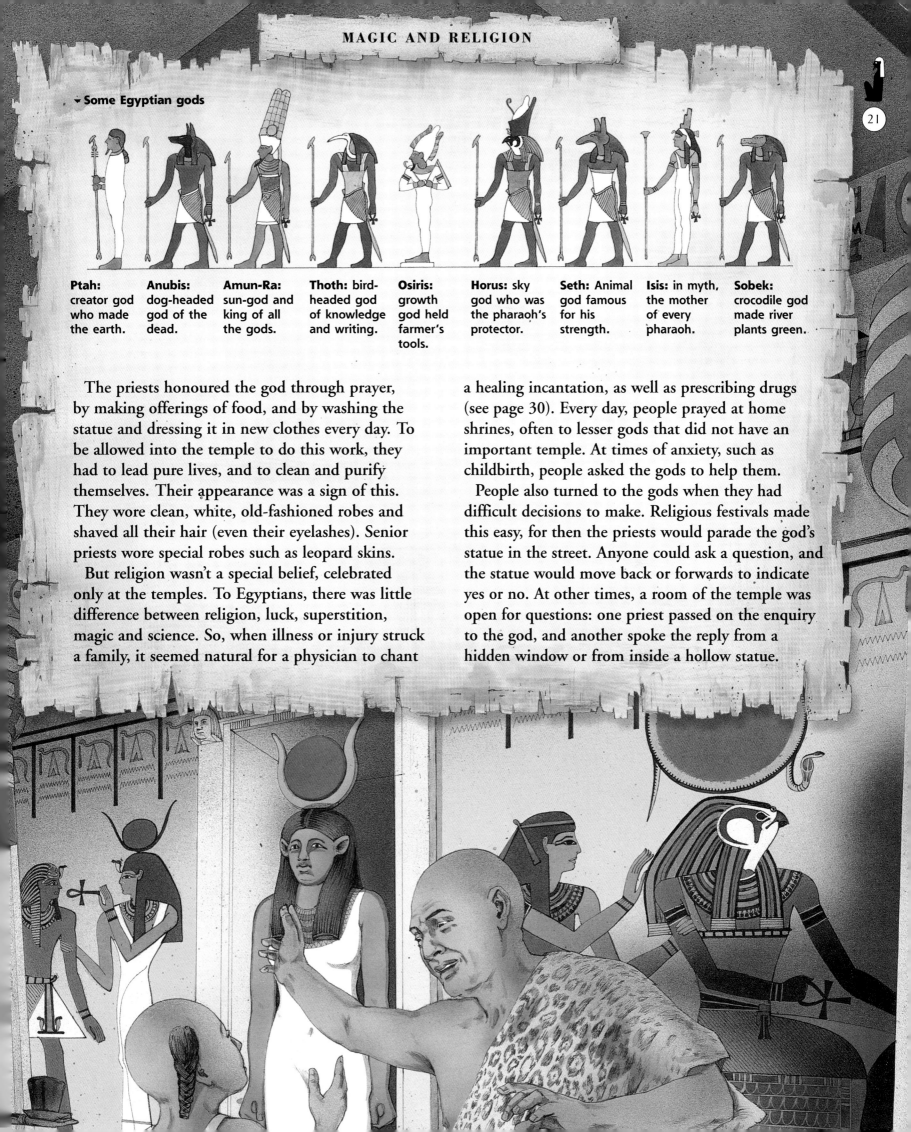

▾ **Some Egyptian gods**

Ptah: creator god who made the earth.

Anubis: dog-headed god of the dead.

Amun-Ra: sun-god and king of all the gods.

Thoth: bird-headed god of knowledge and writing.

Osiris: growth god held farmer's tools.

Horus: sky god who was the pharaoh's protector.

Seth: Animal god famous for his strength.

Isis: in myth, the mother of every pharaoh.

Sobek: crocodile god made river plants green.

The priests honoured the god through prayer, by making offerings of food, and by washing the statue and dressing it in new clothes every day. To be allowed into the temple to do this work, they had to lead pure lives, and to clean and purify themselves. Their appearance was a sign of this. They wore clean, white, old-fashioned robes and shaved all their hair (even their eyelashes). Senior priests wore special robes such as leopard skins.

But religion wasn't a special belief, celebrated only at the temples. To Egyptians, there was little difference between religion, luck, superstition, magic and science. So, when illness or injury struck a family, it seemed natural for a physician to chant a healing incantation, as well as prescribing drugs (see page 30). Every day, people prayed at home shrines, often to lesser gods that did not have an important temple. At times of anxiety, such as childbirth, people asked the gods to help them.

People also turned to the gods when they had difficult decisions to make. Religious festivals made this easy, for then the priests would parade the god's statue in the street. Anyone could ask a question, and the statue would move back or forwards to indicate yes or no. At other times, a room of the temple was open for questions: one priest passed on the enquiry to the god, and another spoke the reply from a hidden window or from inside a hollow statue.

Arts, Crafts and Industry

Egypt's skilled workers laboured in hot, grimy studios making tools and pots for everyday use, and luxury objects for Egypt's wealthy. The best craftsmen earned fame and respect creating unique, beautiful works of art for the pharaoh.

You needed all of your senses for a visit to the craft workers' quarter of an Egyptian city such as Memphis. Metal workers attacked your ears as they beat out copper sheets. The stink of rotting flesh from tanneries assaulted your nose. The roaring furnaces of glass-makers dazzled the eyes and seared the skin, and the smoke from potters' kilns invaded your mouth and lungs.

From this warren of workshops came a vast range of goods. Some, such as leather, copper tools and simple pots, would find their way into the homes of ordinary families. But most were made for the pharaoh's palaces, for the homes and tombs of wealthy nobles, and for the many temples. We know what went on in these primitive factories from the objects that have survived, and from tomb paintings. These often show the process

◄ Tomb painters: artists smoothed rough rock with plaster, then used a grid to guide their painting.

of manufacture like a comic strip, from raw materials to finished product.

In the earliest times, individual craft workers did everything. A potter, for example, dug and prepared the clay, shaped and decorated the pots, and then fired them in a kiln. In time, though, workers began to concentrate on just one part of the process – the bit they did best. These craft workers reached very high standards using the simplest of tools. For example, stone vessel makers used soft copper and flint cutters to make jars so thin that you can see light through them.

Crafts were highly specialized and a worker who mastered one trade would stay in it until he died. Stone tool-makers worked hard rock into razor-sharp

blades used for embalming, and for other
sacred rituals. By the New Kingdom, most
blades for everyday use were of copper.
Metal workers made them by heating
ore (rock containing the metal) to
melt the copper, then moulding
and hammering it to shape.
Jewellers worked with more
precious metals: gold dug from
the desert and, later, imported silver.

Pottery was a lowly craft, though
one of the oldest. From the earliest
times, potters shaped bowls and
jars on simple wheels. They did
not spin them quickly, as today's
potters do, until near the end
of the Ancient Egyptian era.
The kilns potters used to
heat and harden their
work were similar to
those used by glass
makers. Glass
began as a shiny
glaze (finish) on
pots, but it's only
a small step from
glazed clay beads to
making them wholly

◀ **Weavers:** Spinning and weaving were
the only trades in which women
worked, though by the New Kingdom
men were beginning to replace them,
until women made fabric only at home.

▼ **Carpenters:** expert
wood-workers used their
skills to make beautifully
carved funeral furniture
like this shrine.

of pure glass. By the
New Kingdom, glass
workers were skilled
enough to make brilliantly
coloured jars and bottles. Leather
workers turned animal skins into
soft, smooth clothing material and
hard-wearing harnesses for chariots.
Carpenters built everything from front
doors to beautifully decorated chests. Since
Egyptian trees were unsuitable for fine
woodwork, carpenters saved costly
imported timber for their best work,
joining up tiny scraps to make larger
planks. The most respected workers were
the painters and sculptors. Employed by
the pharaoh, many became famous and
wealthy; when they died, some were
buried in tombs almost as grand as
those they had spent their
lives decorating.

Deep inside the craftsmen's quarter
  Ipu dodges heat and sound:
Furnaces that billow flame,
  Deafening hammering all around.
A friendly goldsmith calls her in
  'Your bird was here the other day.
Quite tame it was, ate from my hand.
  My friend the scribe took him away.'

Hieroglyphs

On tombs, temples and columns, parades of people, birds, beasts and shapes recorded stories, spells and messages. Called hieroglyphs and painted by scribes, these signs were Egypt's first written language.

Hieroglyphic writing looks like a jumble of magic signs. How could anybody have remembered what every picture meant, when each word had a different sign? But look closely, and you'll see that some signs appear more often than others: a snake with horns . . . a reed . . . an owl . . . a leg . . . a chick. This is because only the most common words had their own unique signs in hieroglyphic writing. To write less common words, scribes used sound signs, or a kind of picture riddle.

The signs that appear most often are the sound signs. For example, this sign: 🦉 stood for an owl – but more often scribes used it to write the letter 'M'. Not every sound in the Egyptian language had a sign. There were no signs for our vowels. This led to some confusion. For example, if English writing has no vowels, then 'BG' could mean bag, beg, big, bog, or bug. To help the reader understand what was written, scribes added meaning signs.

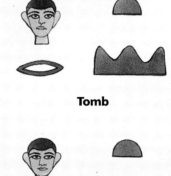

Tomb

Sky

◀ **Meaning signs:** scribes used the same three sound signs to write 'tomb' and 'sky'. To make it clear when they meant 'tomb', they added the sign for a foreign land: 〰️, because Egyptians thought of death as a journey to a distant country. In a similar way, adding the meaning sign for high: ▱, explained 'sky'.

When they came to a word they could not draw, scribes instead drew several words which together sounded like the word they wanted to write. For example, to write the English word 'belief', you might draw a bee and a leaf. If you find this easy to understand, you might have succeeded in Ancient Egypt!

With the cage clutched in her hand
   Ipu's sure her bird she'll trap.
The scribe sits cross-legged on the floor,
   A roll of papyrus on his lap.
'I'm sorry, girl,' he says politely,
   'The bird's not here.' But seeing her sorrow,
He adds: 'I took it to my school —
   You can have him back tomorrow.'

Scribes

The scribes who could read and write were a fortunate few. They were all men, and they got the job because their fathers had been scribes. To write, a scribe sat cross-legged, and stretched across his lap a roll of papyrus – a kind of paper made from reeds. For a pen, he used another reed, either chewed at the end to form a brush, or slit to hold ink. Ink was made from gum mixed with soot to make it black or with red mud to make it red.

Writing was not the only thing that scribes did. They also had many other duties, just like government employees today. They collected taxes. They handed out seed corn for farmers to plant. Surveyor scribes measured the fields. More were in charge of the canals, and every other part of government and the law.

▸ **Rosetta Stone:** the key that unlocked the mystery of hieroglyphs, the Rosetta Stone is now on show in London's British Museum.

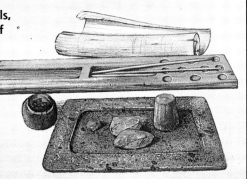

▸ **Writing kit:** inkwells, palettes and rolls of papyrus were a scribe's everyday working tools. A picture of a palette and ink made up the hieroglyphic sign for 'scribe'.

Early in the history of the Nile valley, scribes wrote everything in hieroglyphs. The little pictures were slow to write, and by 2700 BC, scribes had begun to use a quicker form of writing called hieratic. Twenty centuries later, they developed demotic, an even faster way to write. Hieroglyphs continued for monuments, tomb writings and official documents. They finally fell out of use around AD 400. People gradually forgot how to read them, and for centuries scholars puzzled over the meaning of the mysterious little pictures. Then, in 1799, French soldiers uncovered a stone buried at the town of Rosetta, in the Nile delta. It had the same words written in hieroglyphs, demotic and Greek. Scholars understood Greek, and with help from the Rosetta Stone, Frenchman Jean-François Champollion (1790–1832) translated hieroglyphs 23 years later.

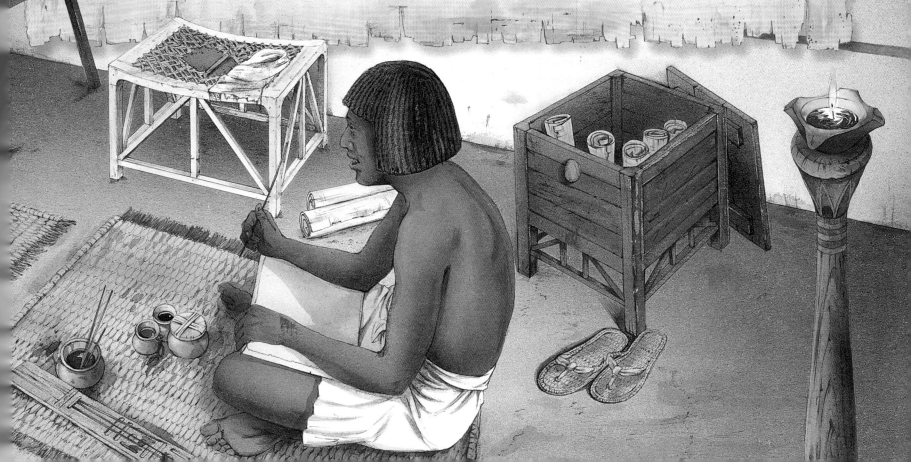

Children

*Most Egyptian children escaped schooling. Instead of studying, they followed
their parents and learned the jobs they would do as adults. Only the sons of scribes
learned to read and write: those who did not concentrate could expect a whipping.*

Childhood in Ancient Egypt was a gradual preparation for the world of grown-ups. Training for work began much earlier than it does today. In the countryside, boys were able to make themselves useful from a very young age. They could scare birds, pick insects from crops, or help with gleaning — collecting spilled grain after the harvest. In a land where farm chemicals and machines were unknown, these simple tasks could make the difference between hunger and plenty. As they grew older, boys copied their fathers' jobs, helping to herd animals, plough and sow seed.

Girls helped their mothers in the home. Poorer parents expected daughters to help out with chores such as milling flour, cooking, cleaning and looking after

▲ **Playtime:** Egypt is a hot country, so children grew up in the open air. Tomb paintings show them with hoops, and playing a piggy-backed ball game.

younger children. In the households of wealthy scribes, slaves did some of these jobs, but girls would still have followed their mothers around the home, watching and copying.

A boy from one of these families had a rather different life. Like his father, he would grow up to be a scribe, so from about the age of nine, he began studying. In the Old Kingdom scribes usually taught their own sons, but later boys studied together at schools. These were probably held out of doors, in the morning cool. Sitting in the shade, boys practised writing hieroglyphs or hieratic. They did not write on papyrus, which was costly, but ostraka (broken pottery bits), flat pieces of stone,

Toys and Games

Childhood wasn't all about work. Tomb paintings show games children played, and the dry air and darkness of tombs has preserved some of their toys. In carefully-drawn scenes, children arm-wrestle, perform acrobatic stunts and play a kind of blind-man's buff. Boys play war-games; girls juggle and ride piggy-back. Some of their toys were similar to the simpler toys that children still play with: dolls, wooden animals, spinning tops, pull-along ships. Ball games were popular, too: archaeologists have found balls made of reeds, linen and leather. Like Ipu, many children kept birds for pets. Hoopoes were especially popular, because they had pretty plumage and could be completely tamed. A few lucky children kept monkeys as pets, but dogs and cats were more common. Cats were especially loved in Ancient Egypt, and some were even mummified when they died!

◄ **Beasts and balls:** the lion toy had glittering eyes made of crystal, and bronze teeth. Pulling the string closed the jaws.

or a flat board coated with white plaster. For most of their lessons they just copied popular sayings, to practice and memorize the hundreds of hieroglyphic signs. To help learn reading, they chanted out loud as they followed the words. It was a dull way of learning, but few boys dared disobey their teachers, for punishment was swift and brutal. An ancient saying advised parents that 'the ear of a boy is on his back, for he only listens when he is beaten'.

Boys and girls usually lived with their parents until they married, or until boys finished studying and began to work. But they stopped being children much sooner. At special ceremonies, they celebrated the end of childhood with a hair cut. Until they were teenagers both boys and girls wore their heads shaved except for a pigtail which hung at one side. Cutting off this 'sidelock' – and starting to wear clothes more often – was a sign that they were entering the adult world.

Ipu creeps into the class
  To find the bird has gone astray.
An empty cage, an open door
  Show how he made his getaway.
The boy who freed it will be whipped
  With a thong of hippo hide.
Ipu doesn't stay to watch —
  She's seen her bird fly past outside.

At Home

Were homes in the Nile valley crowded, smoke-filled, flea-infested dumps?
Or cool, comfortable and perfectly adapted to the heat? We can only guess,
because their mud walls turned to dust long ago.

Unlike tombs, temples and palaces, Egyptian houses were not built to last. Most of what we know about them comes from tomb paintings, and from the remains of houses further out in the desert, where the dryness has preserved the mud bricks.

The poorest Egyptian houses were probably little different from this hieroglyphic sign for a house plan: four walls with a door in one side. Most, though, had at least two rooms: usually a living room, one or two bedrooms, and a kitchen. The kitchen was more like a yard, because it was open to the sky so that smoke and heat from the cooking fire could escape easily.

These simple homes were easily built, using bricks moulded from Nile mud mixed with straw. The straw added strength, and stopped bricks from cracking when they dried in the sun. Builders stacked the bricks into walls, holding them together with more mud. Split palm logs laid across the top of the walls made the roof. A layer of poles, palm leaves and yet more mud sealed it. A coat of whitewash inside and out sealed the surface.

Most doors and windows faced the shady north side, because a cooling breeze blows from this direction. In the spring, a hot desert wind thick with dust comes from the west, so there were no windows on this side. The thickness of the walls absorbed the sun's heat by day, and released it in the cold desert night to keep the family inside snug. In the height of summer, when even the nights were hot, everyone slept on the roof.

▲ **Water garden:** only the rich could afford a pond in their gardens, but the pharaoh's lake was big enough for a procession of boats.

Some workers building houses shout:
      'Come on, we'll catch this bird together!'
One agile fellow jumps up at it
      But ends up clutching just one feather.
Ipu sits unhappily down
      In a fig tree's cooling shadow.
Her feet disturb a sleeping viper
      That sinks its fangs into her big toe.

Roof sleeping area for hot nights

Staircase

Outdoor cooking area

Storage

Living room

Bedrooms

◄ **Mud house:** though mud brick sounds crude, Egyptian builders used it expertly to make comfortable homes that were well adapted to the hot, dry climate. A coat of whitewash inside and out sealed the surface, and killed pests.

Better-off farmers and skilled workers lived in more spacious houses with more rooms. The homes of wealthy scribes were even grander, though still made of mud. The size of the house and details like stone frames for doors and windows were the outward signs of luxury. Inside, these villas had many rooms. The largest was the living room, with a high ceiling held up by tall tree-trunks. All other rooms – as many as 20 – led off this central hall.

Fine homes like this stood in beautiful gardens. All followed a traditional pattern. Enclosing the garden was a wall with a gate. Passing through it took a visitor into a courtyard filled with trees. Another wall – again with a gate – separated the courtyard from an inner garden, also shaded by trees. The inner garden contained a vegetable bed, and perhaps a pond with fish and ducks. A vine shaded the entrance to the house.

Gardens were a great luxury, because it took a lot of work and scarce water to keep them lush and green. They were places to relax and walk in the shade, but they also provided the owner with useful produce. Trees supplied dates, olives, pomegranates and figs. From the flower beds came vegetables and melons, beautiful bouquets for the house, and herbs for medical treatment.

Egyptians loved stepping out of their houses into these green, shady areas, and when they died, they took the garden with them to the afterlife: tombs contain paintings and clay models of lush, neatly tended orchards, flower beds and ponds.

Don't Get Sick!

Without modern knowledge or medicines, Egyptian doctors mostly treated disease by guesswork and magic. They didn't get far by washing patients' eyes with urine and feeding them crocodile dung. But they managed better with wounds and broken bones and even had some success as surgeons.

The best medicine in Ancient Egypt was not to fall ill in the first place! Those who did get sick – and who could afford medical treatment – called for a sunu: a physician. Sunus were highly respected; there were enough of them that some specialized in just one kind of illness or treatment, just as doctors do today. The most famous physicians, those who treated the pharaoh, had titles that advertised their importance. For example, Pepyankh, physician and high priest of the Old

Kingdom, was called 'doctor to the king's belly', 'shepherd to the king's anus' and 'the king's eye-doctor'. He wasn't the first royal doctor we know of: Imhotep (2667–2648 BC), the architect of Pharaoh Djoser's step pyramid (see page 14) was also the king's physician some 4,650 years ago. He was so skilled that just a century after his death, Imhotep was worshipped as a god of healing.

Whether a physician's treatment worked or not depended on what his patient was suffering from. If it was a fracture, patients were lucky, for sunus were quite successful in treating broken bones. They made splints from the bark of trees to keep the broken ends of the bone together. The discovery of many skeletons with neatly healed fractures suggests that this simple treatment worked.

Treatment of disease was not so reliable. Sunus did not know how the body worked, so for most diseases there was little they could do. They tried surgery to cut out tumours (dangerous growths): some tombs contain medical instruments, and papyrus doctors' manuals describe how they used

▲ **Amulets:** made of stone, metal, glass or glazed pottery, these charms were supposed to guard the wearer from ills. Some were shaped like the body part they protected.

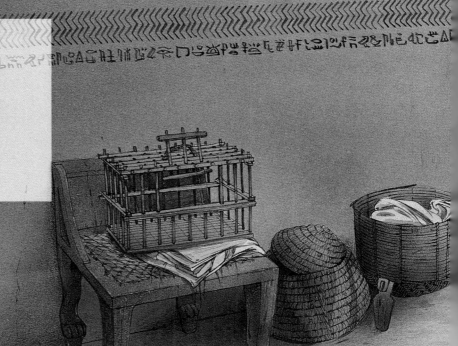

Swelling up to twice its size
    Her toe's a nasty shade of red.
The doctor says: 'You'll do just fine —
    But only if you stay in bed.'
Before she sleeps, she spreads some grain
    Hoping it will lure her bird.
She's woken by its hooting song —
    The sweetest sound she's ever heard!

▸ **Eye of Horus:** according to Egyptian myth, the god Horus was wounded in the eye in a fight. He was cured by the god Thoth, and the eye became a powerful sign of healing.

them. One advises surgeons to heat medical instruments before using them to cut flesh. The idea was to stop bleeding, but this would also have sterilized the knife, reducing the chance of infection.

Egyptian doctors used up to 700 different medicines. Many of them were herbal cures, and a few might have been effective. For example, the poppies they used contain a powerful painkiller, and willow leaves are a source of the same chemical as modern aspirin. Some cures would have done nothing, however: a baldness remedy contained black snake fat, a rook's spine bone and the ash of an ass's hoof. A few must have actually made a patient's health worse. Prescriptions included urine, and the dung of pelicans, crocodiles, flies, lizards – even children. Why did Egyptian doctors use these disgusting substances? Precisely because they were so nasty. The

horror they caused gave them a special, magical power. Medicine and magic were hard to separate in Ancient Egypt. Physicians believed that when devils were causing the illness, they might leave the patient's body if they were sufficiently disgusted.

Doctors and patients believed that magic could work in other ways to bring good health. Both the sick and the well wore amulets. These were lucky charms with special shapes or engraved with magic signs, such as the eye of the god Horus: 𓂀. This belief in the protective ability of magic signs or objects continues to this day, far from the Nile's ancient land. Mediterranean sailors still paint the 'magic eye' on their boats, and many of us wear a rabbit's paw or a magnetic bracelet in the hope that it will bring us good health or good luck.

◂ **Healing powers:** Hesy Re, who lived around 2600 BC, was the world's first known dentist, a scribe, and another of Pharaoh Djoser's physicians (see page 30). He was buried in a magnificent tomb at Saqqara.

Index

ST. ALOYSIUS SCHOOL
220 N. HANOVER STREET
POTTSTOWN, PA 19464

ST. ALOYSIUS SCHOOL
220 N. HANOVER STREET
POTTSTOWN, PA 19464